THE ROYAL AIR FORCE BENEVOLENT FUND

INTERNATIONAL AIR TATTOO 95

RAF FAIRFORD 22-23 JULY

**THE BEST IN
MILITARY AVIATION**

THE ROYAL AIR FORCE BENEVOLENT FUND

ISBN 1 899808 15 9

INTERNATIONAL AIR TATTOO 95

CONTENTS

Introduction	3
Flying Display	9
Victory Finale	36
SkyTanker 95	39
Participating Air Arms:	
Royal Air Force	47
Royal Navy	51
Ministry of Defence/Defence Research Agency	52
Royal Australian Air Force	54
Belgian Air Force	54
Brazilian Air Force	55
Bulgarian Air Force	55
Canadian Armed Forces	56
Czech Air Force	57
Royal Danish Air Force	58
Royal Danish Army & Naval Aviation	59
Finnish Air Force	60
French Air Force	60
French Navy	61
French Army Aviation	62
German Air Force	63
German Army Aviation	64
German Navy	65
Italian Air Force & Army Aviation	66
Royal Jordanian Air Force	67
Royal Moroccan Air Force	67
NATO	68
Royal Netherlands Air Force & Navy	69
Royal New Zealand Air Force	70
Royal Norwegian Air Force	70
Polish Air Force	71
Portuguese Air Force	71
Royal Saudi Air Force	72
Slovak Air Force	73
South African Air Force	74
Spanish Air Force	74
Swedish Air Force	75
Swiss Air Force	76
Turkish Air Force	77
United States Air Force	78
United States Army	82
United States Navy	83
United States Marine Corps	83
Civilians	84
Visitors	86
Struts, Wires and Wingwalkers	88
IAT95 Aircraft Checklist	91

Published by

The Royal Air Force Benevolent Fund Enterprises Publications Unit, Building 15, RAF Fairford, Glos GL7 4DL, England

Publishing Director: **Paul A. Bowen**
Head of Publishing: **Phil Coulson**

Editorial Assistant: **Gary Lane**
Caption Research: **Phil Henden**
Photography: as credited
Cover artwork: **Wilfred Hardy** GAvA
Design: **Graham Finch Design**
Colour repro: **Adroit Photo Litho**
Printed in Hong Kong

ISBN 1 899808 15 9

USAF U-2Rs from the 9th RW on detachment to RAF Fairford continued operations in the days leading up to the weekend airshow, and provided an aircraft for the static display. Peter R March

INTERNATIONAL AIR TATTOO 95

THE BIGGEST AND BEST YET!

Right from the first planning meeting for International Air Tattoo 95 there was a feeling abroad that this show was really going to hit the mark. Sponsorship and participation interest were strong, there were new ideas to be tried, and the essential IAT volunteer team was raring to go. A major factor in the optimistic outlook was the tremendous co-operation of the United States Air Force, IAT's hosts at RAF Fairford, who gave full support in spite of needing to maintain the OL/UK U-2R operational flying commitment right up to and including the weekend of the Tattoo. The fact that IAT was in its third successive year at Fairford was also of considerable benefit, and increased familiarity with the layout of the airfield helped the Logistics and Site Teams in particular.

As always, it was important to adopt the right themes for the world's largest military air display, and avoid the danger of IAT simply being a procession of fast jets with full 'burner and lots of noise. That suits some, of course, but an aim for IAT 95 was to attract the family and

provide for them a spectacle of aircraft and flying that would stay in the memory for a long time. Also, 1995 saw the 50th anniverseries of peace in Europe and the Pacific, and by the time of IAT the nation had already seen many events at which their respects could be paid. When IAT 95 was nominated as the Royal Air Force's official Victory Airshow, the pressure came on to provide a flying tribute worthy of such an historic occasion.

The plan that encompassed all the aims of IAT 95 was ambitious, but all who attended agreed that a new standard was set, with no other airshow able to compete in terms of sheer size, spectacle and entertainment – a true theatre of the air. The excellent spell of hot, dry weather with cloudless blue sky spanned the whole week of IAT activity, bringing its own problems regarding fire hazard and, for the volunteer teams, raging thirst, but also providing the best conditions for photography that IAT has seen for a long time. The Park and View facilities were hectic from the Wednesday prior to the show weekend

This South African Air Force Boeing 707-344 was a welcome newcomer to IAT 95, forming part of the SkyTanker line-up. A Colcombe

right through to the departure of the last aircraft on the following Monday.

The operational theme of IAT 95 was SkyTanker, and on Wednesday the inbound procession of mighty tankers began. In a role where the types of aircraft used are limited, there was a great variety of paint schemes and national markings amongst the impressive line-up of 707 variants, whose crews showed great interest in each other's aircraft and, of course, the pristine VC10 K4. Flanked by the giant Tristar KC1 and KC-10A at the eastern end, and at the western end by a Canadian KCC-130H and a Royal Saudi Air Force KC-130H, the Boeing line-up was truly impressive. The first appearance in the UK of a South African Air Force Boeing 707-344 of 60 Sqn excited a lot of attention, and it became one of the most photographed aircraft at the show.

Once all the tankers were in position and their crews enjoying the professional seminar and fellowship for

which IAT is famous, the rest of the static display was put into place by the tireless ground engineering team. The use of cones and rope to barrier the aircraft proved to be much easier to erect than steel barriers, and they provided a less intrusive appearance to the public. A large canvas fort was erected on the northside of the airfield in preparation for the re-enactment of the historic Hendon Pageants and Displays, one of the other themes for IAT 95.

Other SkyTanker aircraft on show included a Royal Air Force VC10 K4 (below) and a French Air Force C-135FR (right). Daniel March/Gordon Bartley

The Sir Douglas Bader Trophy was awarded to the Czech Air Force Mi-24 *Hinds* for a thrilling display routine. Daniel March

The first Royal Air Force airshow was staged at RAF Hendon on 3rd July 1920, and the International Air Tattoo can trace its ancestry to that occasion. The attack on the fort by easy-to-watch-and-follow vintage biplanes proved to be exactly the sort of flying that many parents and children had come to see, and the newly-provided family picnic areas were packed with enthralled spectators. The modern equivalent was superbly demonstrated by Jaguar and Harrier aircraft, and the Hercules tactical demonstration with its spectacular Khe San approach and landing was as popular as ever.

While all the flying was going on, the hospitality chalets and Patron's Pavilion were catering for record-breaking

The *Patrouille Suisse* returned to IAT 95 with Northrop F-5Es having replaced the familiar Hunters. Daniel March

numbers. The special enclosure for the Friends of IAT, and the Grandstand seating area proved their worth again, and many of the superb photographs in this book were taken from those areas. A particularly special enclosure at IAT 95 provided stylish refreshment and hospitality for a large number of veterans of the Second World War. Sponsored and provided by SAGA, the title sponsors of IAT 95, the facility was enormously successful, particularly because of the view it provided of the Victory Finale.

For many of the volunteers and staff at IAT 95, the heat, thirst and tired feet all became worthwhile when they saw the reaction of the veterans to the Victory Finale. As wartime aircraft pulled up in the traditional 'missing man' salute, unashamed tears coursed down proud cheeks as veterans remembered the thousands of their colleagues who never returned. The tribute was all the more moving for the tremendous line-up of modern

Also from the Czech Air Force, *Team Duha* made their IAT debut flying Sukhoi Su-22 *Fitters*. Daniel March

The spectacular Victory Finale was a fitting tribute to the fallen of World War II. Peter R March

This tiger-striped Norwegian Air Force F-5A and Czech Air Force *Hind* formed part of the Victory Finale line-up. Keith Gaskell

military aircraft on the runway, all adding their own salute as the hovering helicopters gradually climbed and the strains of Sunset and The Last Post died away. It was a Finale worthy of the memory of all those airmen and women who were engaged in conflict fifty years before.

So whether it was for the satisfaction of the flying professional, the aviation enthusiast, the family who wanted a good day out or the dignified veteran lost in memories, IAT 95 hit the mark. With more than 400 aircraft on the ground, and more at Brize Norton and Rendcomb, IAT 95 was the biggest yet. The limits of Fairford's considerable capacity for aircraft have been fully explored and probably reached! A new standard has also been set for a thoughtfully planned display, and families have never had so many individual attractions to fill their day. Can the International Air Tattoo get any better? Join us in 1996 for the Silver Jubilee International Air Tattoo on 20 & 21 July, again at RAF Fairford, and see for yourself.

This year, an invitation was extended to all who attended IAT 95 to submit their best photographs of the show for possible publication in this book and the prestigious IAT Calendar. The response was excellent, as was the general standard of photography. Many of the photos on the following pages were taken by our regular volunteer photographic team, but many others were taken by enthusiasts who were in the right place at the right time. To all who submitted their pictures, a very big 'Thank you', and if your contribution has not been used this year, try again in '96!

This German Air Force MiG-29A *Fulcrum* was displayed next to a USAF F-15E Eagle. Stephanie Foster

A pair of USAF B-52H Stratofortresses and a B-1B Lancer dominate this view of just part of IAT 95's extensive static display. Peter R March

Flying display participant was this Italian Army Agusta A129 Mangusta. Gordon Bartley

Making its IAT debut was this two-seat Harrier T10 from the A&AEE. Gordon Bartley

With their national colours adorning the underside of their wings, the *White Iskra's* TS11 aircraft are seen in beautiful weather conditions opening Saturday's show. Using coloured smoke to full advantage and making their first ever UK public display at Fairford, the Polish Air Force flew a very smooth display.

Peter R March & Brian Strickland

FLYING DISPLAY

The Slovak Air Force *White Albatros* team never manage to display against blue skies at IAT. Their routine was still impressive, though, and here the L-39Cs are seen taxiing in after their display on Sunday morning. John Dunnell

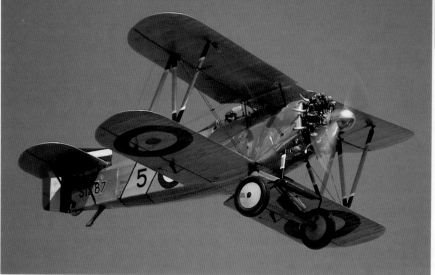

Although the Hendon Air Pageants were already a thing of the past when the Shuttleworth Trust Gloster Gladiator (above) and John Fairey's replica Fairey Flycatcher (left) first took to the air, the spirit of those early days was recaptured by the biplane duo.

Andrew Roberts

Always popular with the IAT crowds, the Stearmans of the Crunchie Flying Circus gave their customary polished performance. The wing-walking routine is reminiscent of the old barn-storming days and is particularly enjoyed by the young children who sometimes find military jet noise a bit much! Andrew Roberts

The St Ivel Antonov An-2 was Utterly Impossible to miss as it sedately sailed across the airfield on Saturday, reappearing on Sunday to land. Some thought that it had taken that long to complete a visual circuit, but really it returned to Rendcomb on Saturday.
M Bratnell

There was a Fairey Swordfish II from the Royal Navy Historic Flight seen on both days of the Tattoo, but they were different aircraft. W5856 flew on Saturday, and the display on Sunday was given by LS326, both aircraft transitting from their base at Yeovilton.
Andrew Roberts

The SABENA Old Timers Lysander IIIA wears the markings of No 161 Squadron Royal Air Force and is registered in Belgium as OO-SOT. Ben Dunnell

The British Aerial Museum's beautifully restored Blenheim IV Z5722 (G-BPIV) and British Aerospace's Mosquito RR299 (G-ASKH) teamed up for a nostalgic formation flypast. Peter R March

The Royal Netherlands Air Force *Grasshoppers* based at Deelen near Arnhem have now been display flying for 22 years with their venerable Sud Alouette IIIs. All pilots are instructors with 299 Squadron which carries a 'Grasshopper' motif in the Squadron Badge, hence the team's name.

Peter R March & Maxwell Knowles

The immaculately finished aircraft of the Royal Jordanian Air Force Historic Flight displayed on both days of the Tattoo, operating from Bournemouth International Airport. The aircraft carry British civil registrations – Vampire FB6 G-BVPO, Vampire T55 G-BVLM, and pristine Hunter T7 G-BOOM – and are operated on behalf of the RJAF by Jet Heritage. Daniel March & Peter R March

The partially-open canopy on the Jet Provost Club's Jet Provost T3A bears witness to the searing temperatures at IAT 95. Formerly XN461, this venerable JP spent most of its life being thrashed by earnest young trainee pilots, and must now really enjoy being flown smoothly and precisely as i displays to an appreciative audience. Peter R March

BAe Hawk T1 XX235 of No 19(R) Squadron and its pilot Flt Lt Don Ritch won the Steedman Display Sword for Best UK Display. Both pilot and aircraft came from the RAF's Flying Training School at RAF Valley in North Wales. Together with the 'spare' No 19(R) Sqn Hawk, XX235 also took part in the spectacular Victory Finale.

Peter R March, Brian Strickland & John Dunnell

Seen finishing off their punchy display routine by igniting flares, this unique display given by the Czech Air Force's *Team Duha* (Rainbow) flying Sukhoi Su-22 *Fitters* proved to be one of the highlights of IAT 95's flying programme. The team is led by Lt Col Jaroslav Kankia aged 37 from 32/1 Squadron based at Namest Nad Oslavou.

Peter R March, Rob Holder & Gordon Bartley

In all, an amazing total of 14 DH 82A Tiger Moths were seen at Fairford over the weekend. G-AKXS and G-AJOA (T5424) took part in Saturday's display, and were replaced by G-AGEG and G-BPHR (A17-48) for Sunday's flypast as part of the stunning Finale. A once-in-a-lifetime treat was enjoyed by representatives of each of the wartime Commands when they flew into Fairford from Rendcomb in the Tiger Moth fleet.

Necessary safety regulations do not allow tanker aircraft to display with receivers actually connected, but the Harrier GR7s of No 1 Sqn were as close to the No 101 Sqn VC10s as they could have been without being plugged in. The VC10 in grey finish, ZA149, is a K3 variant, whilst the hemp-coloured tanker is VC10 K4 ZD240. Peter R March

Providing a really majestic flypast, Tristar C2 ZE706 was closely followed by VC10 C1K XV103 of No 10 Sqn on Saturday. The next day saw the same No 10 Sqn aircraft, but No 216 Sqn was represented by Tristar ZE705. John Chase

Five Lockheed C-130 Hercules of Lyneham Tactical Wing took part in the flying display, which included a CIK variant demonstrating its in-flight refuelling role. Known as 'Albert Formation', these Hercules came from Nos 24, 30, 47, 57(R) and 70 Squadrons. Andrew Roberts

Just as the re-enactment of the old Hendon Air Display attraction of bombing the fort was enormously popular with the IAT95 crowd, so the display of modern close-support aircraft capability provided a great spectacle. Harrier GR7s streaked in to simulate the delivery of their ordnance, and Fat Albert showed that he can be surprisingly nimble when operating in the tactical role. Combined with lots of noise and smoke, this part of the Tattoo proved particularly memorable for most of the crowd.

M Schenk, Ben Dunnell & Mark Lopak

AMX Centaur MM7131/RS13 from the Italian Air Force Test School at Practica di Mare flew a very tight aerobatic display, its pilot keeping the AMX within the confines of the airfield. Peter R March & Daniel March

Interest in the flying display programme sometimes wanes for tired and hungry visitors, but the unmistakable roar of a 'Hoover-Jet' in the hover is always enough to have them scrambling for a better view. The solo Harrier GR7 display at IAT 95 was flown by Flt Lt Andy Offer of No 20 Sqn who treated his audience to a great display and tons of dust! Peter R March

Above: To the disappointment of some of Saturday's visitors, the Royal Moroccan Air Force Display Team *Marche Verte* only flew on Sunday to demonstrate another legacy of Hendon – aircraft tied together in formation. The brightly-painted CAP 231s flew a spirited routine with plenty of smoke, and landed with wing-tips intact!

Peter R March & Daniel March

First displayed to the UK public at IAT in 1987, the *Patrulla Aguila* with their seven Casa 101 Aviojets have since returned to every IAT at Fairford to thrill the crowds. All pilots who fly with the team are instructors at the Spanish Air Force Air Academy at San Javier near Murcia.

Everyone who saw the Italian Air Force Aeritalia G222 perform a barrel-roll during its display turned to the person next to them to confirm what they had seen. The agility of this aircraft was quite amazing, and pilot Major Luca Rizzi of the Reparto Sperimentale Volo based at Practica di Mare, Rome, certainly put it through its paces. Ben Dunnell

Displaying for the very last time at an IAT event, Royal Air Force Search and Rescue Wessex HC2 XT601 of No 22 Squadron based at RAF Valley is due to be replaced by the Westland Sea King. Daniel March

The three Czech Air Force Mil Mi-24D *Hinds* of 331 'Tiger' Squadron based at Prerov provided an exciting display routine before a finale which consisted of each one dropping flares. The team went on to win the Shell UK Oil Sir Douglas Bader Trophy for the Best Flying Display.

M Schenk, Mike Kerr & Daniel March

Below: Team leader Lt Col Stefan Jasso (left) and the other team members at the presentation of the Shell UK Oil Sir Douglas Bader Trophy. Peter R March

At the height of their very busy season, the *Red Arrows* had other commitments on both days of the Tattoo and did not land at Fairford. Their 1995 display sequence was as impressive as ever, and included a perfect Viggen formation and, for the crowd, heartstopping crossover manoeuvres by the synchro pair. Led by Squadron Leader John Rands, the *Reds* celebrated their 30th birthday during the 1995 season.

Rob Holder

The essential blue sky for *The Falcons* Parachute Display Team to really show their talent was in abundance on both days of the Tattoo. As with many jobs done by true professionals, the routine was made to look quite easy in spite of quite strong winds above 1000 feet.

Martin Cleaver

The striking all-black finish of this No 16(R) Sqn Jaguar GR1A from RAF Lossiemouth looks just as good upside down as it does the right way up. Sporting the Saint emblem that perpetuates the name by which No 16 Sqn has been known since it formed at St Omer in France in 1915, the all-black finish of XX116 is reminiscent of other types that No 16 Sqn painted black in their operational days, including a certain Buccaneer in Germany....!

Peter R March

Amongst several Tornado displays was one flown by GR1 ZA560 of the Tri-national Tornado Training Establishment at RAF Cottesmore. All conversion training for the ground attack variant of the Tornado is undertaken at Cottesmore for crews from Germany, Italy and Britain.

Aldo Wicki & Mike Kerr

One of the most striking colour schemes at IAT 95 was sported by this Tornado F3 of No 56(R) Squadron based at RAF Coningsby. Usually the well-known Phoenix emblem and red-and-white checks quickly denote a No 56(R) Sqn aircraft, but with the stylish flashes on wings and tailplane there was definitely no mistaking who owned this one!

Mike Kerr & Peter R March

Below: It was a proud moment in the International Air Tattoo's distinguished history when Eurofighter 2000 made its first UK public appearance at IAT 95. Although the display profile was somewhat restrained because EF2000 has not yet completed all the trials of its revolutionary fly-by-wire flight control system, the agility and power of this latest thoroughbred were obvious to all. The full display routine is eagerly awaited, and may even be seen at IAT 96. P Bunch

Following the retirement of the Hawker Hunter from Swiss Air Force service, the *Patrouille Suisse* returned to IAT this year with six gleaming F-5E Tiger IIs that were flown with great precision. The team is led by Captain Freddi Ramsier, who is joined this year by Grego Tschudi '2', Paul Thoma '3', Markus Thoni '4', Werner Hoffman '5' and Daniel Hosli '6'. The team is based at Dubendorf Air Station near Zurich.

John Chase, Brian McKay, Andrew Roberts & A Ord

Flying a very impressive display in his MiG-29A *Fulcrum* (0619), Maj Ivan Hulek, aged 35, of the 1st LETKA 'Tiger Squadron' based at the 31st Air Base at Sliac, won this year's Superkings Trophy, presented by Imperial Tobacco for the best overall Solo Jet Display.

S Screech & Peter R March

The award of the Superkings Trophy to Maj Hulek was made by the Director of IAT, Paul Bowen. Peter R March

Representing the Hashemite Kingdom of Jordan, the *Royal Jordanian Falcons* are now in their third season flying the German Extra 300 special performance aerobatic aircraft and, under the leadership of Omar Hewaig, won the Lockheed Martin Cannestra Trophy for Best Aerobatic Display at IAT 95. The team is fully supported by King Hussein of Jordan who has watched many of their displays since their IAT debut at Greenham Common in 1979.

John Dunnell, Ben Dunnell & Peter R March

The French Air Force Dassualt Mirage 2000C of EC2/2 Cote d'Or Squadron, from Dijon-Longvic, gave a truly magnificent display which consisted of high speed turns and some breathtaking aerobatic sequences.
Rob Holder

Using smoke to good effect, Capt Ries 'Champ' Kamperman, aged 32, a Weapons Instructor with 312 Squadron, Royal Netherlands Air Force, was the only pilot to display the F-16 at IAT 95. Flying a specially painted aircraft (J-508), his display was rounded off by a slow speed high-alpha pass, displaying well the F-16's fly-by-wire capability.
Peter R March

The sheer grace of Concorde's flight, and the fascinating predatorial look it has as it settles onto the ground, make this beautiful aircraft impossible to ignore. The excitement of taking a charter flight into or out of IAT is now a regular feature, but everybody gets a thrill from seeing this masterpiece of aviation engineering, whatever the angle.
J Thompson

Right: Long-time participants at IAT, the Army Air Corps' *Blue Eagles* helicopters from Middle Wallop always have something different for their audience to admire. While the split-second timing of the Gazelle AH1 formation is a delight to watch, the antics of the singleton Lynx AH7 wreathed in coloured smoke (below) leave enthusiasts looking forward to the *Blue Eagles* show once the AAC takes delivery of new, more agile, battlefield helicopters! G W Butler

Above: Specially constructed for the snap manouevres of a truly aerobatic aircraft, the Walter Extra 300s of the Rover Display Team flew some classic sequences in which the g-forces, both positive and negative, must have placed tremendous demands on the endurance of the pilots. The Rover Team operates out of Denham Airfield, Buckinghamshire. Peter R March

Left: Colourful Swiss-built Pilatus PC7 L-02 belongs to the Royal Netherlands Air Force Training Unit EMVO based at Woensdrecht. Peter R March

Lacking the bulk of the Hind, the Agusta A129 Mangusta ground attack helicopter of the Italian Army Aviation still presented a very menacing appearance as it demonstrated the tactical flying techniques necessary to survive and operate on the modern battlefield. Peter Hilton & Daniel March

Below: Full reheat was used to great effect by Tornado IDS 45+36 of the German Navy, seen about to take-off to begin a powerful display, with the specially constructed fort forming the backdrop. Peter R March

Above: Representing the Swedish Air Force in the flying display, pilot Ken Lindberg is seen displaying a Saab SF37 Viggen from F7 Wing. Ken has over 1200 operational flying hours on the Viggen and will soon be training on the JAS 39 Gripen fighter.
Aldo Wicki & Daniel March

Right: Some aircraft have an engine note that is unmistakable, and the Shorts Tucano T1 is one of them. The aircraft displays very nicely, though, and this machine from 1FTS, RAF Linton-on-Ouse, provided a fine performance in the capable hands of Sqn Ldr Mike Johnson. Peter R March

Enthusiasts and would-be experts now spend many hours discussing the various merits of the world's premier air display teams. Most would agree that the big-team performances have reached a difficult-to-exceed degree of excellence, and the show put on by the *Patrouille de France* on Saturday was brilliant. The Alpha Jet E aircraft are based at Salon de Provence, and the team was led at IAT 95 by Major **William Kurtz.** Peter R March

Using their rich coloured smoke to full advantage, the *Frecce Triccolori*, a component of the combat capable 313 Gruppo based at Rivolto near Udine, Italy, returned once again to IAT. Now in their 40th year of Air Demonstration Flying, the team has flown Aermacchi MB339As since 1981. Matthew Hill

Undoubtedly one of the most-photographed aircraft at the Tattoo, the USAF Rockwell B-1B Lancer of the 37th BS/28th BW carried the nose art 'Brute Force'. Captain Jim Weigle flew the powerful bomber, which is based at Ellsworth Air Force Base, Texas. M Schenk & Aldo Wicki

As speculation over its possible successor continued, Nimrod MR2 XV232 from Kinloss went through the routine that has impressed airshow crowds the world over. Built to tolerate the turbulence of long, low-level tactical manouevring over the Atlantic, the Nimrod is nevertheless agile and powerful. As the aircraft pulls up steeply at the end of its display, the Flight Engineer fires a green flare from the Verey pistol mounted in the flight deck roof.

Daniel March & Peter R March

The pilots of the Royal Navy's Helicopter Display Team, *The Sharks*, are all instructors from 705 Naval Air Squadron at RNAS Culdrose. Their stated intention is to demonstrate the excellent manouevrability of the Gazelle HT2 and, without doubt, they fulfil their aim. This year, the *Sharks* have a Royal Australian Navy exchange officer as a team member for the first time.

Anne Henderson

The Veterans' podium was the focal point of the amazing aerial tribute to the fallen airmen of WWII. Such a finale to an air show has never been seen before, and there was hardly a dry eye amongst the many veterans who received this massive salute.
Daniel March

The cream of modern air power lined the runway as helicopters rose behind them in salute, awaiting the flypasts that would symbolise missing men.
Peter R March

First came the Tiger Moths, 12 of them gently rising and falling as the formation epitomised the fragility of man's mastery of the air.
Brian Strickland

Then came the Lancaster, Spitfire, Hurricane and Mosquito formation (above), the Spitfire pulling up into the heavens to symbolise the departure of fallen airmen. American wartime aircraft were represented by a B-17 flanked by a P-38 Lightning, P-47 Thunderbolt and P-51 Mustang (right), with the Mustang pulling up into the missing man manouevre. Peter R March

The reconciliation of countries now allied together in NATO was demonstrated by four German Air Force Tornados in formation, one aircraft pulling up to honour fallen Luftwaffe colleagues. Peter R March

As the *Red Arrows* synchro pair flashed in from East and West to crossover and pull up to write a huge 'V' in red smoke, a Mustang, Spitfire and Bf 109 roared overhead from the South to break through the 'V'. Peter R March

After a brief silence of remembrance, fireworks filled the sky with noise and smoke (left) adding to the tremendous noise of the aerial salute, and then the B-1B Lancer (below) flown by Captain Jim Weigle thundered past, wings swept, to conclude the flying display. Peter R March, Keith Gaskell & Ben Dunnell

SKYTANKER MEET

The operational theme is always an important element of the International Air Tattoo, bringing together professional aviators from a particular flying discipline to discuss their role with fellow flyers from other countries. IAT 95 provided the forum for air-to-air refuelling specialists to meet for SkyTanker 95. High-ranking representatives of many of the world's major air arms and defence industries, as well as the numerous operational aircrews, attended a seminar and competitions based on skills relevant to the Skytanker theme. For the general public, of course, SkyTanker 95 provided the opportunity to see airborne tankers from all over the world, and few will forget the sight of all those Boeing tankers lined up in impressive array at IAT 95!

Below: Eight USAF Boeing KC-135s came to Fairford to support the SkyTanker 95 Meet, creating an impressive line-up of tails and refuelling booms.
Keith Gaskell

Above: The impressive SkyTanker line, headed by a French Air Force C-135FR. Peter R March

Inset above: Together in the massive SkyTanker 95 static park were these two Commonwealth Boeing 707 tankers from the South African Air Force and Royal Australian Air Force Rob Holder

SKYTANKER MEET

The VC10s and Tristars that comprise the Royal Air Force tanker force impressed the professional and public visitors alike. So different from the Boeing 707 derivatives, the elegant lines of the VC10 belie its age, just as the current colour schemes of No 101 Sqn aircraft belie their varied histories. Since the demise of the Victor tankers, whose contribution to the air war in the Falklands conflict was incalculable, the VC10s of No 101 Sqn and the Tristars of No 206 Sqn have proved themselves worthy successors by their contribution during the Gulf War. The 'shiny tens' of No 10 Sqn, also based at Brize Norton in Oxfordshire, can now add their weight to the tanker effort when required, giving the RAF an enviable flight refuelling capability.

Gordon Bartley, Peter R March & Daniel March

Providing an ABC of international tankers at IAT 95 were aircraft from Australia, Brazil and Canada. The Royal Australian Air Force sent a Boeing 707-338C of 33 Sqn (above), the Brazilian Air Force provided a KC-137 from 2/2GT (left), and the Canadian Forces were represented by an immaculate CC-137 of 437 Sqn (below).

Peter R March & Ben Dunnell

SKYTANKER MEET

Above: Giving a bit of the 'French Connection' to SkyTanker 95 at Fairford, this very rare Boeing C-135FR of ERV 93 'Aunis' based at Istres-Le-Tube, arrived on the Friday afternoon for the static display. There are currently twelve CFM 56 engined C-135FRs which form part of the French Air Force's tanker force supplemented by C-160NG Transalls, two of which were also present at IAT 95, one as a SkyTanker 95 static exhibit (below) and the other as support aircraft for the Alpha Jets of the *Patrouille de France*. Daniel March & D D Ramsay

SKYTANKER MEET

Not to be overlooked in the SkyTanker Meet was the Italian Air Force Tornado MM7057/36-54 of 36° Stormo which was equipped with a buddy-buddy refuelling system. Soph Moeng

Below: Italian Air Force Boeing 707 328B MM62148 14-01, of 14° Stormo based at Practica di Mare. Rob Holder

Below: There were many marks and variants of the ubiquitous Lockheed Hercules at IAT 95. Royal Saudi Air Force KC-130H 3202 of 32 Sqn based at Riyadh formed part of the SkyTanker 95 Meet.
Daniel March

SKYTANKER MEET

Amongst the more exotic tankers to arrive at Fairford on Wednesday 19 July was this Royal Saudi Air Force Boeing KE-3A of 18 Sqn based at Riyadh. Peter R March

Right: The first appearance in the UK of South African Air Force Boeing 707-344 AF617 of 60 Sqn excited a lot of interest, both when it arrived on Wednesday and again when it departed for its Waterkloof base on Monday. Nigel Bassett

Good nose art always draws attention, and the 'Nightmare' artwork adorning USAFE KC-135R 63-8008 of the 100th ARW was no exception.
Buedts Dirk & Peter R March

SKYTANKER MEET

Left: The USAF's 319th ARW was represented by KC-135R Stratotanker 64-14837 from Grand Forks AFB, North Dakota.
Peter R March

Right: USAF KC-10A Extender 83-0079 of the 305th AMW dominated the eastern end of the SkyTanker line-up, and being close to the RAF Tristar provided an interesting comparison of the two tri-jets.
Peter R March

Above: Boeing KC-135E 57-1512 'Bad Boy' from the 452nd AMW USAF Reserve based at March AFB, California. Buedts Dirk

Right: Overall Winner of the coveted Concours d'Elegance competition was Boeing KC-135R 59-1444 'Spirit of Rickenbacker' of the 166th ARS, Ohio Air National Guard.

SKYTANKER MEET

Departing Fairford on its homeward journey, AFRES KC-135R 62-3530 of the 434th AMW was heading for Grissom AFB. Daniel March

Right: One of the last SkyTanker participants to arrive, KC-135E Stratotanker 59-1457 of the Pennsylvania Air National Guard brought in several USAF veterans to enjoy the Tattoo and was awarded a Special Mention in the Concours d'Elegance.

Peter R March

The United States Marine Corps sent three Hercules to IAT 95 as participants in the SkyTanker meet; a pair of KC-130Rs, including 160625/BH from VMGR-252 (left) and a KC-130F from VMGRT-253.

Brian Strickland

BAe Harrier T10 ZH654 is currently operated on test and trials with the A&AEE at Boscombe Down. These conversion trainer Harriers are now replacing the older T4s, the first being delivered to No 20 Reserve Squadron, the Harrier OCU, at RAF Wittering in 1994.
Richard Matthews

Left: Chinook HC2 ZA709 of No 7 Sqn flew in from Odiham to take part in the static display. The downwash from these powerful helicopters makes them unsuitable for flying display participation.
Brian Strickland

Below: The 1FTS Shorts Tucano T1 ZF406 from Linton-on-Ouse was one of three that flew in, and it looked extremely sleek in the all-blue colour scheme it was sporting.
Brian Strickland

Based at RAF Lossiemouth and used in the low-level anti-shipping role, Tornado GR1B ZA456 of No 617 Sqn is seen here departing on the Monday after its appearance in the static display. Daniel March

Left: Attracting attention with its Italian markings, Tornado F3 ZE340 from RAF Coningsby's No 56(R) Sqn is part of the programme to augment the Italian Air Force air defence strength until EF2000 enters service.

Daniel March

Westland Wessex HC2 XR511 is one of ten such helicopters that equip No 60 Sqn at RAF Benson in Oxfordshire. Primarily committed to supporting the Army's 5 Airborne Brigade, No 60 Sqn's Wessex also see a lot of service in Ireland.

Brian Strickland

Since the disbandment of No 42 Sqn at RAF St Mawgan, all the RAF Nimrod MR2 aircraft are based at RAF Kinloss in Scotland. XV251 may well be back at IAT 96 when the operational theme will be SeaSearch.

Daniel March

Above: Always popular with the crowd, the Harrier line-up comprised four GR7s and a GR7 replica. The aircraft came from No 1 Sqn, No 3 Sqn and the Strike/Attack Operational Evaluation Unit based at Boscombe Down. Daniel March

Right: Jaguar GR1A XX766/EA of No 6 Squadron (the 'Flying Canopeners') taxies in on arrival. The squadron forms part of the Coltishall Jaguar Wing and has been operational on the Jaguar since 1974. Peter R March

Right: A regular participant in the static display at Fairford, No 6 FTS sent Jetstream T1 XX482 from RAF Finningley.The aircraft is flown by the Multi Engine Training Squadron of which No 45 (Reserve) Squadron is a component. Peter R March

Left: The white triangle on its fin helps to identify this Tornado as a GR1A of No II(AC) Sqn, RAF Marham, where it operates in the reconnaissance role. Brian Strickland

Thirty years have elapsed since the faithful HS Dominie T1 entered RAF service with No 1 Air Navigation School at Stradishall. Since that time countless navigators have completed their early training on the Dominies which are currently flown by 6FTS at RAF Finningley.
Rob Holder

Right: Colourful in comparison with the other RAF Hawks that participated in the 21st birthday celebrations at Fairford, BAe Hawk T1 XX172, resplendent in its Welsh dragon artwork, comes from RAF St Athan's Station Flight. Situated in Mid Glamorgan, Wales, St Athan is reponsible for all Hawk servicing as well as other RAF types.
Rob Holder

Below: No 8 Squadron Boeing Sentry AEW1 ZH104 seen here wearing 80th anniversary markings is one of seven Airborne Early Warning aircraft based at RAF Waddington, Lincolnshire. The squadron was formed at Brooklands on 15 January 1915. Rob Holder

Above: Parked in the helicopter static display, Westland Sea King HAR5 XV666 CU-823 of 771 Squadron Royal Navy, is based at RNAS Culdrose in Cornwall, in the Search and Rescue role.
Daniel March

Right: Hawk T1A XX346 is flown by the Fleet Requirement Air Defence Unit, often acting as opposition for the training of the Navy's Harrier pilots. At IAT 95 it was on static display. Peter R March

Left: 771 Naval Air Squadron fly Sea King HAR5 XV666 in the rescue role, and it acted as a vital medical evacuation standby facility throughout the International Air Tattoo, parked to the north of the runway. Brian Strickland

The elegant Hunters based at Boscombe Down are always a welcome sight at IAT. Hunter FGA9 XE601 (left) is flown by the A&AEE, while Hunter T7 XL612 (below) is operated by the Empire Test Pilots School.

Peter R March & Daniel March

A&AEE Jaguar T2A ZB615 used the northern taxyway to evaluate its port mainwheels. One wonders if the pilot is suggesting the engineers put the flat bit of the tyres at the top of the wheels so he can continue to taxy?

John Dunnell

Above: Fast becoming a rarity, with only a handful left in UK military service, DTEO Canberra B2 WH734, now 41 years old, started its operational life back in 1954 and is employed as a target tug aircraft at its Llanbedr base in Wales. Rob Holder

Right: Andover C1PR XS596 flies from Boscombe Down in support of the 'UK Open Skies' mission, the on-going disarmament verification programme. Brian Strickland

The ETPS Advanced System Training Aircraft (ASTRA) Hawk is currently being used to evaluate fly-by-wire systems such as that used in the new Saab Gripen fighter.
P Thompson

ROYAL AUSTRALIAN AIR FORCE

Just about to touch down on Wednesday afternoon, the furthest-travelled participant at IAT 95 was Boeing 707-338C A20-627 of 33 Sqn, Royal Australian Air Force. Peter R March

BELGIAN AIR FORCE
(Force Aérienne Belge/Belgishe Luchtmacht)

Alpha Jet AT31 of No 7 Squadron, Belgian Air Force was finished in an eyecatching colour scheme to celebrate the unit's 45th anniversary. The unit is a component of 9 Wing based at Brustem/St. Truiden Flying Training School. A closer look at this aircraft's tailboom reveals the names of the crew responsible for designing the paint scheme on this immaculately turned out aircraft. P Hollands

BRAZILIAN AIR FORCE
(Forca Aerea Brasileira)

The crew of Brazilian Air Force KC-137 2402/02 really entered into the spirit of things, and having sported their national flag with such pride then had a hard job preventing its 'liberation' by equally enthusiastic crews from other nations! Brian Strickland

BULGARIAN AIR FORCE
(Bulgarski Vozdusny Vojski)

What must rank as one of the rarest participants at IAT 95 was this Tupolev Tu-134A *Crusty* LZ D 050 of the Bulgarian Air Force's 1st Regiment based at Dobroslaviza Sofia.

Daniel March

CANADIAN ARMED FORCES
(Forces Armées Canadienne)

Above: The pure white finish on this Canadian Forces CC-137 of 437 Sqn really shows off the beautiful lines of the Boeing 707 design. P Bunch

Not quite so elegant, but a welcome visitor to the SkyTanker Meet, was Canadian Forces KCC-130H Hercules 130342 of 435 Sqn, seen here on departure from Fairford.
Daniel March

(Ceske Vojenske Letectvo)

Antonov An-30 *Clank* 1107 operates with No 344 Squadron of the Czech Air Force at Pardubice Air Base as an 'Open Skies' aircraft and for this role it carries special cameras including infra-red line-scanning equipment and complex radar systems.

Rob Holder & Thomas Bisson

Also from Pardubice Air Base, Antonov An-26 *Curl* 2409 formed part of the static display and is shown here on departure for its home base. Daniel March

ROYAL DANISH AIR FORCE
(Kongelige Danske Flyvevaaban)

Seen departing from Fairford, multi-mission Gulfstream III F313 belongs to the RDAF Transport Eskadrille 721 based at Vaerløse near Copenhagen. Three of these aircraft undertake the roles of Search and Rescue, Fishery Protection and Fast Jet Communications for Tactical Air Command Denmark (TACDEN), with detachments also being made to Sondrestrom Air Station in Greenland. Rob Holder

Left: C-130H Hercules B-680 of Eskadrille 721 came to Fairford from Vaerløse for the static display, and departed for Alborg on Monday.
Daniel March

Right: Royal Danish Air Force F-16B ET-197 belongs to Eskadrille 726 based at FSN Alborg. This unit now undertakes the photo-reconnaissance role with specially adapted 'photo-recce' pods which can be fitted to the underside of the F-16. Daniel March

ROYAL DANISH ARMY & NAVY

(Haerens Flyvetjaeneste / Søvaernets Flyvetjaeneste)

IAT is always well supported by the Danish Armed Forces, and the helicopter static display was enhanced by three helicopters from the Royal Danish Army. The 1st RDAAC sent two SA550C-2 Fennecs, P-369 (left) and P-287, which is used by their VIP Flight. Hughes 500M H244 (below left) is flown by the 2nd Royal Danish Army Air Corps. Soph Moeng

Two helicopters from the Royal Danish Navy appeared in the static display. Lynx Mk 80 S-142 came from Eskadrille 722 based at Vaerløse, who also provided an S-61A Sea King.

Brian Strickland

FINNISH AIR FORCE
(Suomen Ilmavoimat)

An extremely welcome visitor to IAT 95 was this Finnish Air Force Hawk T51 (HW-315) from the Finnish Flight Test Centre based at Halli. This aircraft joined the 21st birthday celebrations in the static park, underlining the Hawk's international sales success. Finland ordered 50 Hawk T51s in 1980. Pete Webber

FRENCH AIR FORCE
(Armée de l'Air)

Supporting the French *Patrouille de France* aerobatic team, this C-160NG Transall transport aircraft was parked on the north side of the airfield and, therefore, not readily seen by many. F208/64-GH is flown by the French Air Force 64th Air Transport Squadron (ET/64) based at Everux. Brian Strickland

French Navy Lynx HAS2(FN) 623 was one of the many helicopters that provided the spectacular backdrop for the Victory Finale. Operated by 34F based at Brest it was parked northside for the duration of the Show. Tony Wood

Falcon 10MER 143 is flown by the Navy's ES57 on communications duties, and is seen here arriving at Fairford from its base at Landivisiau to take part in the static display. Daniel March

Amongst the heavy helicopters in the static display was SA321 Super Frelon 164 of the French Navy's 32F based at Brest. The unit operates Super Frelons for SAR and transport duties.

Soph Moeng

FRENCH ARMY AVIATION
(L'Aviation Legère de l'Armée de Terre)

Wearing standard French Army colours with high visibility dayglo panels, this Cessna F406 Caravan II 0010/ABN is one of a pair operated by 3 GHL Armee de Terre as a target towing and communications transport, based at **Rennes St. Jacques.** Daniel March

French Army Air Corps AS532 Super Puma 2282/AIS (left) and SA342M Gazelle 4166/CXA (below) made the journey from Phalsbourg in Southern France where they are part of the Fourth Air Mobile Division.
Daniel March & Brian Strickland

GERMAN AIR FORCE
(Luftwaffe)

Above: A Friday arrival from Koksijde, German Air Force UH-1D 71+73 from LTG-62 is based at Wunstorf, Germany and was a rotary participant in the Victory Finale. Brian Strickland

Right: Seen departing on Monday for Leck, German Air Force C-160D 50+06 from LTG 63 was on static display. Daniel March

Specially marked German Air Force Alpha Jet 41+09 from Furstenfeldbruck made a pleasant change from the more usual green camouflage schemes carried.
Daniel March

GERMAN AIR FORCE
(Luftwaffe)

German Air Force F-4F Phantom 37+38 of JG73 joined the two Turkish F-4Es in the static park at IAT 95. Note the dayglo orange tail this aircraft wears which enables other German F-4F crews to keep a check on who's who during fast and furious dogfight scenarios against each other. The Luftwaffe is set to keep its F-4F Phantoms in service until at least the year 2000 when the Eurofighter EF2000 will be made available as a replacement. Rob Holder

GERMAN ARMY AVIATION
(Heeresflieger)

One of two German Army helicopters to attend IAT 95, CH-53G 84+84 is seen arriving from Rheine-Bentlage, home of 15 Regiment. Also in the static display was MBB Bo 105M 80+24 from the same regiment.

Ben Dunnell

GERMAN NAVY
(Marineflieger)

Right: German Navy Sea King Mk41 89+67 was parked in the static display over the weekend of IAT, having flown from its base at Kiel-Holtenau. It is operated by MFG5 as a long range Search and Rescue helicopter.
Ben Dunnell

MFG 2 is now the sole Tornado unit in the German Navy, and three of its aircraft attended IAT 95, with one taking part in the flying display. 46+20 arrived for the static display on Friday from Eggebek. Peter R March

Left: German Navy Do 228 57+01 from MFG-5 seen landing at Fairford after its flight from Nordholz.
Daniel March

Largest of the German Navy participants was maritime patrol Atlantic 61+14 based at Nordholz with MFG-3.
P Thompson

ITALIAN AIR FORCE & ARMY
(Aeronautica Militare Italiano)

Based at Grosseto near Sienna, two Italian Air Force TF-104G Starfighters of the 4° Stormo/20 Gruppo (MM5425/4-34 and MM5461/4-42) appeared in the static display. Their aircrews were warmly received by many aviation enthusiasts as the Starfighter is now becoming a rarity, the Italian Air Force being the only F-104 operator left in Europe. Soph Moeng

Right: Newer additions to the Italian Air Force inventory on static display included two MB339As from 61° Stormo at Lecce, MM54463/61-17 shown here and MM54496/61-42. A third MB339A from the *Frecce Tricolori* (MM54473/4) was also on view. Daniel March

ITALIAN ARMY
(Aviazione Leggera dell'Esercito)

First time visitors to IAT at RAF Fairford were the Italian Army. AB-412 MM81360/EI-469 is seen arriving prior to taking up its position in the static display. Daniel March

ROYAL JORDANIAN AIR FORCE

(Al Quwwat Al-Jawwiya Al-Malakiya Al Urduniya)

A regular participant at IAT is one of four Lockheed C-130H Hercules of the Royal Jordanian Air Force, and seen here is 346 inscribed 'Guts Airline'. This unusual name was given by King Hussein of Jordan in recognition of 3 Squadron's Hercules crews who have undertaken hazardous missions in support of UN Forces in Bosnia and Croatia.

Peter R March

ROYAL MOROCCAN AIR FORCE

(Al Quwwat Al-Jawwiya Al-Malakiya Marakishiya)

A display team not seen at IAT for several years, the Moroccan *Marche Verte* made a welcome return to Gloucestershire skies, bringing CN-235 CN-AMB as their support aircraft. Brian Strickland

Above: Leaving the runway at Fairford, Boeing 707 TCA LX-N19996 of the Nato Airborne Early Warning Force from Geilenkirchen AFB in Germany, acts as a training aircraft for the multi-national crews who are posted to the force from their respective NATO air forces. The Boeing 707s (of which there are three in service) can operate as logistics support for the Boeing E-3A fleet when deployed to forward operating locations in Greece, Turkey and Norway.
Rob Holder

Always easy to spot in the static display, the Boeing E-3A makes a useful meeting point for visitors to such a large event, in this case NATO's LX-N90443. The crew are always primed for the many questions from the crowd about the strange radar dish perched above the aircraft. Peter R March & Daniel March

ROYAL NETHERLANDS AIR FORCE
(Koninklijke Luchtmacht)

Regular supporters of the Tattoo are F-16s from Holland. F-16A J-021 and F-16B J-068 of 312 Sqn, Royal Netherlands Air Force depart back to their base at Volkel. Daniel March

Right: Having replaced the Alouette III in the SAR role, Rescue Flight Agusta-Bell AB 412 R-03 made the long trip to IAT 95 from its base at VLB Leeuwarden in northern Holland. P J Hall

ROYAL NETHERLANDS NAVY
(Marine Luchtvaartdienst)

Lockheed P-3C (Update II) Orion 304 of 320 Squadron Royal Netherlands Navy is seen departing Fairford for its base at Valkenburg. It is one of 13 Orions operated by the Maritime Patrol Wing (MARPAT) and all have been in service since 1982. Daniel March

ROYAL NEW ZEALAND AIR FORCE

Not quite ready for the long trip home to New Zealand, C-130H NZ7004 from 40 Squadron prepares to depart for RNAS Culdrose to take part in another airshow.
Peter R March

ROYAL NORWEGIAN AIR FORCE
(Kongelige Norske Luftforsvaret)

Above: A Tiger unit since 1977, 336 Skvadron, Royal Norwegian Air Force operate this F-5A, based at Rygge. Three more F-5s joined this 'Tiger' in the massed Victory Finale, commemorating the part played by Norwegian pilots who served alongside RAF squadrons in Britain during WWII. Pete Webber

Left: Operated by 719 Skvadron, Royal Norwegian Air Force are four DHC-6 Twin Otters including 7057, seen parked in the static display at IAT. It had flown from its base at Bodo, situated in the Arctic Circle. Soph Moeng

POLISH AIR FORCE
(Polskie Wojska Lotnicze)

A first time visitor to IAT was Antonov An-26 *Curl* SP-KWC as part of the Polish Air Force debut onto the UK airshow scene. Daniel March

PORTUGUESE AIR FORCE

(Força Aérea Portuguesa)

Although being gradually replaced by the F-16, the A-7P remains in front line service with the Portuguese Air Force. Twin-seat TA-7P 15546 from 304 Squadron at Monte Real is seen awaiting the arrival of its crew for the flight home. P Claydon

Portuguese Air Force C-130H-30 Hercules 16806 belongs to Esquadra de Transporte 501 based at Montijo Air Base, and supplements the five other standard C-130Hs that form the backbone of heavy-lift operations in support of Portuguese and UN Forces deployed overseas. R Clayton

ROYAL SAUDI AIR FORCE
(Al Quwwat Al-Jawwiya Assa'udiya)

Above: A part of the impressive display from Saudi Arabia, and attending the SkyTanker Meet was KC-130H 3202 from 32 Squadron based at Riyadh. This aircraft previously carried the serial 457 but changed as part of a renumbering scheme requiring the squadron number to be the first part of the aircraft serial. Rob Holder

Parked near the UK and German Tornados in the static display, this Tornado IDS (762) belongs to 7 Sqn, Royal Saudi Air Force. It flew into Fairford before returning to Saudi Arabia after maintenance at BAe Warton. Daniel March & Ian Grainger

Operation
Desert Storm
"THE GULF WAR"
Royal Saudi Air Force
7th Squadron

Tornado IDS 762

ROYAL SAUDI AIR FORCE

Seen arriving at IAT95, Antonov An-12BP 2209 acted as support transport for the large Slovak Air Force contingent which attended IAT 95, coming from the 1st Dopravna Letka (Transport Wing) based at Piestany Slovakia. A closer look at the tail revealed the 'rubbed out' former Czech & Slovak markings. John Chase

Another Slovak Air Force participant seen arriving at IAT is MiG-29UB *Fulcrum* 1303 from 1 Squadron. John Chase

SOUTH AFRICAN AIR FORCE
(Suid Afrikaanse Lugmag)

Underneath a beautiful blue sky, the nose profile of South African Air Force Boeing 707 AF617 of 60 Squadron bears its unit badge containing the very appropriate motto of 'Accipmus Et Damus' (Pride in Excellence), as the crew were awarded the 'Spirit of the Meet' Graviner Trophy and also the British Aerospace Defence Trophy as Overall Winner in the ground competition. K A Tappenden

SPANISH AIR FORCE
(Ejército Del Aire Español)

A very rare visitor to the static display at Fairford was C-130H T.10-04 of Escuadron 311, a component unit of the 31 Transport Wing based at Zaragoza, which flew as support aircraft for the seven Casa 101 Aviojets of the *Patrulla Aguila*. Gordon Bartley

(Svenska Flygvapnet)

Wearing a very attractive airline style livery, Saab Tp 100 (SF340) 100001 belongs to F16 Wing and is based at Uppsala in the communications role. In fact, the Swedish Air Force are developing an AEW version of the Tp 100 to work alongside Sweden's new generation multi-role fighter, the JAS 39 Gripen. Daniel March

Left: Acting as support for the four Saab Viggens at IAT 95, C-130H/Tp 84 Hercules 841 operates with the same wing as the fighters and is based at Satenus-Tun.

Daniel March

Together in the static park, two Swedish Air Force Saab Viggens from F7 Wing based at Satenus-Tun flew into Fairford with two others, which were parked on the northside flightline.

F7 Wing was the first Flygvapen unit to operate the Viggen back in 1973 and is currently working up on the Swedish Air Force's new light attack fighter, the JAS 39 Gripen.

Pete Webber

Once the mount of the *Patrouille Suisse*, Hunter F58 J-4025 was donated by the Swiss Air Force to The Royal Air Force Benevolent Fund following the re-equipment of the team with the F-5E. The Swiss Air Force was the last major operator of the Hunter and although a few examples have been retained in storage in Switzerland, the vast majority have been distributed to museums and a number of private operators. Daniel March

Regular visitors to IAT will be familiar with the Swiss Air Force's Dubendorf-based Learjets which fly into Fairford before and after the show in a support capacity for the *Patrouille Suisse*. Seen from the forward door of its partner, Learjet 35A T-782 is parked on one of the north side dispersals with T-781 providing the photographer with his foreground. Aldo Wicki

TURKISH AIR FORCE
(Türk Hava Kuvvetleri)

Silver Turkish Air Force Lockheed C-130E Hercules 13186/12-186 operates with 222 Filo at the 12th Air Base Erkilet (Kayseri), and delighted enthusiasts with its rare visit to IAT. Gordon Bartley

Baring their teeth in the static display were two F-4E Phantoms of the Turkish Air Force, still retaining their original 'Egyptian 1' camouflage which was used by their previous owners, the Missouri Air National Guard. These two examples came from the 1st Air Base Wing at Eskisehir and are operated by 112 Filo 'Seytan' Squadron.

Daniel March & Ben Dunnell

A regular visitor from the East coast of the United States, C-5B Galaxy 87-0031 is based at Dover Air Force Base. As part of the 436th AW it provides airlift support for the United States Air Force, Army, Navy and UN in many different theatres.

Brian Strickland

Left: Always popular with the crowd, even more so in the rain, the C-5B demonstrates its cavernous interior.

Peter R March

Above: From the 37th Bomb Squadron at Ellsworth AFB South Dakota, this B-1B Lancer is prepared for its flight in the Victory Finale. Brian Strickland

In its forty-first year, the C-130 maintains its position at the top of the airlift world. C-130H 92-0550 of the 50th AS begins its Atlantic crossing back to Little Rock, Arkansas, where it is part of the 314th Airlift Wing. Daniel March

Right: Not the usual transport of the Flying Doctor, but this C-9A Nightingale provides vital aeromedical support for the United States Air Force in Europe. Based at Ramstein with the 75th Airlift Squadron, 71-0880 is one of a number of adapted DC-9 airliners used to transport sick servicemen to and from treatment centres. Daniel March

C-141B Starlifter 66-0201 arriving at Fairford from March AFB, California where it serves as part of the Air Force Reserve with 452 AMW. Ben Dunnell

Above: Boeing B-52H 60-0058/MT is seen moments before touchdown at Fairford, which is no stranger to the occasional detachments of B52s that are deployed there on exercise. However, this B-52H of the 5th Bomber Wing based at Minot AFB North Dakota had flown down from Keflavik in Iceland on the conclusion of exercise 'Northern Viking' 95. In company with a USAF Reserve B-52H, it joined a B-1B Lancer (right) in the static display. Ben Dunnell & P Bunch

USAF(E) F-16C Fighting Falcon 88-0413/AV belongs to the 510th Fighter Squadron of the 31st Fighter Wing based at Aviano, Northern Italy. Named 'Buzzard 01', it is the mount of the 510th FS 'Boss', and is seen departing Fairford on the Monday after the show.
Daniel March

Inches off arrival at IAT, F-15E Eagle 90-0248 is the mount of the Wing Commander of the 48th Fighter Wing at Lakenheath.
Daniel March

Right: Now part of a European based mixed fighter wing, these USAF(E) A-10As Thunderbolt IIs of the 81st FS are seen shortly after arrival on the static display ramp. They share Spangdahlem Air Base in Germany with F-15s and F-16s, and form part of the 52nd Fighter Wing.
Nigel Bassett

U-2R 80-1092 on home ground at Fairford, with a protective shade over the cockpit. The distinctive lines of this high level reconnisance aircraft have become a regular sight since the move of the European base of the 9th Reconnaissance Wing from RAF Alconbury to Fairford earlier this year. Peter R March

Another special role aircraft was EC-130E 63-7773 from the 193rd Special Operations Squadron based at Harrisburg International Airport, Pennsylvania. This squadron is part of the Air National Guard who have become regular participants at IAT since its early days. Spectators were able to view some of the specialised equipment fitted within the EC-130E. Soph Moeng

Departing for Wiesbaden, Germany RC-12K 85-0155, part of the US Army's 1st Military Intelligence Battalion, carries a large number of specialist aerials that supply the electronics suite on this aircraft.
Daniel March

Right: Soon to become a familiar sight in the UK following the British Army's selection of the Apache as its new anti-tank helicopter, AH-64 86-8941 is based with the US Army at Illesheim, Germany. Soph Moeng

Left: US Army UH-60A 88-26083 belongs to the 158th Aviation Regiment. The Black Hawk forms the backbone of the utility helicopter fleet of the US Army, serving American forces around the world. Buedts Dirk

Part of the European Command transport fleet is UH-1H 74-22513 based at Stuttgart, Germany. In conjuction with a number of C-12s and C-21s, the unit is responsible for the transportation of senior officials through the European Theatre of Operations.
Peter R March

UNITED STATES NAVY

Leaving Fairford's runway on departure, this US Navy F/A-18C Hornet of VFA-87 was the only aircraft of its type to appear at IAT 95.
Peter R March

UNITED STATES MARINES

A rare participant from the West Coast of America was KC-130R 160240 from VMGR-352 based at El Toro Marine Corps Station, California. A participant in the SkyTanker Meet, the aircraft is used for the aerial refuelling of the rotary and fixed wing assets of the US Marine Corps.
Daniel March

Another tanker from the States was KC-130F 150687/GR, this example being based at Cherry Point Air Station, North Carolina. It serves with VMGRT-253, the squadron responsible for training all crews that fly the C-130 with the Marines.
Daniel March

CIVILIANS

Left: Part of Pilatus Britten Norman's demonstration fleet, the bulbous-nosed BN-2T Islander G-BVHX arrived at the show on the Friday in formation with Defender 4000 G-SURV. Daniel March

Above: Looking extremely realistic, this replica British Aerospace Hawk 200 was at Fairford as part of the Hawk's 21st Anniversary celebrations.

Brian Strickland

Below: The immaculate Dragon Rapide G-AEML outside the SAGA Veterans Enclosure made a pleasant contrast to the modern military hardware on view at IAT 95. Daniel March

With certainly the shortest journey home, ex-Royal Air Force Whirlwind HAR10 XJ729 is operated by local enthusiasts from the nearby village of Cricklade.

Peter R March

CIVILIANS

The Royal Air Force's first jet trainer was the Jet Provost T1. Recently restored to flying condition and operated by Kennet Aviation, T1 G-AOBU was formerly used as a company demonstrator by Hunting Percival and took part in celebrations marking the 40th anniversary of jet trainers. Ben Dunnell

Right: A later model of the Jet Provost, T5 XS230 (G-BVWF) provided an interesting comparison with the T1 in the static park. Once operated by the Empire Test Pilots School at Boscombe Down, it is now privately owned and flown from Cranfield in Bedfordshire. Peter R March

Left: Departing from RAF Fairford on the Monday morning in the capable hands of the Chairman of the IAT Flying Control Committee, Group Captain Geoff Brindle, Vampire T11 U-1219 (G-DHWW) from the Source Classic Jet Flight at Bournemouth Airport. Daniel March

Below: Kennet Aviation's well maintained Gnat T1 XM693 (G-TIMM), based at Cranfield, was a participant in the Rolls-Royce Jet Trainer Anniversary display. Peter R March

Above: Czech Air Force Tu-154 B2 *Careless* 0601 of 3 DVLP based at Prague-Kbely is always kept very busy before and after IAT events flying in support of the Czech Air Force contingent. This year's Czech participation involved no less than ten aircraft.

John Chase

Seen parked on the operational north side of the airfield is the second of two Antonov An-26 *Curl* support aircraft for the Polish Air Force aerobatic team the *White Iskras*. SP-LWA was previously operated by LOT, Poland's national airline.

Gordon Bartley

BAC 1-11 XX 105 from the Defence Research Agency was used to ferry aircrew between Fairford and Boscombe Down.

John Chase

Empire Test Pilots School Gazelle HT3 XZ939 ferried crews from Boscombe Down for the various Ministry of Defence aircraft on static display. P J Hall

Right: Bringing in sponsors and organisers of Holland's Airshow Europe 96 was the immaculate F-27 PH-KFG of the F-27 Friendship Flight Association, based at Schipol.

Chris Lawrence

VIP transport for senior German Air Force visitors to IAT 95 was this rarely seen VFW 614 of Special Air Transport Wing. 17+03 arrived and departed on the Friday before the show, and was followed the next day by visiting German Air Force LET 410 53+11.

Richard Matthews

'STRUTS, WIRES AND WINGWALKERS'
— A look back at airshows over the years by Reg Moody —

The delightful Dorset town of Christchurch has many tangible links with our history, including its 900 year old Priory which survived King Henry VIII's anger against the church. The town nestles against the much larger historic town of Bournemouth. It was close to the border of these two towns that modern history was to be made in tragic circumstances. As part of Bournemouth's Centenary celebrations, a cleared area in Southbourne, a suburb of Bournemouth close to the historic Hengistbury Head that overlooks Christchurch, was turned into an airfield for one of the first airshows seen in this country.

It was windy on July 12 1910 as hundreds of awed spectators gazed skywards at these new flying machines that defied all the rules of gravity as they swooped, turned, climbed and dived under perfect control, or so it seemed. The pilots could be seen sitting among the struts and wires out in the open, heavily protected in leather coats, scarves and helmets or caps as they nursed the unpredictable engines and controls of their aircraft.

As a group of machines swept in competition across the airfield, one of Britain's pioneer flyers, The Hon Charles Stewart Rolls, was struggling with his Wright aircraft in the stiff wind which hit him beam on during a tight turn. As his flimsy machine turned, two rear rudders, only recently fitted to the original Wright design, broke loose from the framework, the wires controlling them catching in the chain and propellers. In seconds the stricken aircraft dived from a hundred feet to the ground. Charles Rolls, Britain's first air crash victim, died. Few then could have realised that his name would be etched on the cowlings of mighty jet engines, decades later, in a lasting tribute to one of Britain's first pioneers of the air. In his short life Rolls was the first Englishman to fly with the legendary Wilbur Wright, and the first person to complete a two-way crossing of the Channel. Almost 72 years on from that fateful day in 1910, a Mach 2 Concorde made four low level runs in front of another air show crowd at Hurn, overflying the spot where Rolls had crashed in a flying machine barely capable of matching the speed of a modern car.

For several years the International Air Tattoo was held at Greenham Common. A line-up of Phantoms dominated the static display in 1983. Graham Finch

Although the 1914-18 war was soon to stop in its tracks the development of display flying, it speeded up the development of aircraft and the numbers being produced. From a handful of aircraft flying at the time of Rolls' fatal crash, by 1918 a separate air arm, the Royal Air Force, had been formed and its strength was an amazing 22,647 aircraft including 103 airships. The RAF had 133 Squadrons, 15 Flights overseas and more than a quarter of a million personnel. Once the war was over, the public's curiosity about men and machines that defied gravity had been stimulated to epic proportions by the exploits of the 'aces' of the air.

When wars are won the first target of the politicians seeking economies, at least in democracies, is the armed forces, and in Britain this was not slow in coming. The junior Service was quick to realise that it would now have to compete with the Army and the Navy for a slice of the Defence budget cake and used modern PR tactics to keep itself in the public eye. A number of wartime pilots, back earning a living, found a profitable and enjoyable outlet for their flying skills by giving local displays and private flights almost anywhere in the country where a flat piece of grass could be found. The growth of air displays that had begun at Bournemouth in 1910, was underway. These young men became known as barnstormers, a title imported from the United States where the spectacle of daredevil flying was already very popular.

The RAF, too, was not slow to see the PR potential in this activity both for its need for public support and its growing demand for new young blood to form its post-war aircrew numbers. On July 3 1920, the first air display of the pattern still used today was held at Hendon airfield north of London, and was an instant success. Known first as the RAF Tournament, then as the Aerial Pageant and finally as the Hendon Display, this show continued annually until 1937 when the RAF, already reduced in strength, was so busy training to prepare for the danger looming from central Europe that it could no longer support the effort involved. However, local RAF shows, known as Empire Air Days, continued until four months before the Second World War began, by which time the number of stations opened to the public had grown to sixty with an annual attendance of one million.

By the end of the Second World War in 1945, the RAF strength had grown to 55,469 aircraft and the names of Spitfire, Hurricane, Mosquito and Lancaster were household words. The politicians were soon at it again, cutting the Services to the bone, but this activity was soon halted as it became clear that the Communists had no intention of either disarming or reducing expansionist policies. The danger of heavily cutting the RAF was highlighted by the Berlin Airlift which stretched its scarce resources, especially in transport aircraft and, more crucially, trained personnel.

As the RAF began to shape its peacetime role in the face of such threats, it found itself desperately short of recruits, especially aircrew. The modern jet aircraft coming into service demanded much higher grade pilots than previously, and some training difficulties existed in converting newly trained pilots from piston-engined aircraft to high-speed jets. For a time, until suitable advanced jet trainers arrived, pilots had to bridge the gap from initial trainers to Meteor jets by flying Spitfires. What was urgently needed was a massive PR campaign to find sufficient volunteers to enable aircrew selection in particular to be highly selective. Advertising was useful, but demonstration and visual impact were the tried and tested tools of the 'recruiting sergeant' as the Hendon displays had demonstrated. The prestige won in the Battle of Britain provided the key and soon the RAF was mounting annual 'At Home Days' to celebrate Battle of Britain Week. Nearly all operational and training stations opened their doors, demonstrating their own local role but stimulating general interest by using visiting aircraft, exciting 'set-piece' displays and aerobatic performances. This positive approach proved highly effective, and aircrew applications soon began to climb.

At this time rivalry began to develop between the more successful RAF stations such as Biggin Hill, North Weald, Finningley and Scampton, who had to report, at the end of their open days, the attendance figures. Because of its close connections with the Battle being commemorated, and because it was near to the London defence correspondents and photographers, Biggin Hill led the field from the beginning. No systems were in place to correctly compute the actual attendance figure, since no entry charge was made except for car-parking. It became, then, a somewhat humorous competition between Station Commanders who were ultimately responsible for the figure telephoned to Air Ministry for onward transmission to the

At the International Air Tattoo at Greenham Common in 1976, a total of 27 Hunters formed an impressive line-up to mark the 25th anniversary of the type, with the famous all-red prototype WB188 forming the centrepiece of the display. Graham Finch

media. Various methods were used to try and be accurate, such as consultation with the police and transport companies, and by visual assessment of the crowds on a comparison basis from the previous year, but wild exaggeration was rife.

For many Station Commanders the main target was to knock Biggin Hill off the top, and the figures climbed each year to quite unbelievable levels. One fighter base commander was prone, when asked for his final figure, to look at the previous totals, then at the police and transport assessment, take a sweeping glance at the size of the crowd from the top of the flying control tower and then, holding a wet finger into the wind, solemnly pronounce the official figure!

It was soon obvious that as the RAF, like the other Services, began to run-down, and as a large proportion of its strength moved to German bases, the number of these annual Battle of Britain shows had to be reduced. And Biggin Hill itself was losing much of its operational use, being finally reduced to the home of the Officer and Aircrew Selection Centre and, for a short while, a University Air Squadron. But it was very important that the major Battle of Britain Air Show should continue at Biggin for as long as possible. It was, from the public point of view, the symbol of the Battle, it had the famous Chapel within its boundaries and, by its nearness to London, also embraced the memories of the steadfast civilian stand against the Nazi bombers. For the same reasons it attracted a larger crowd than any other station. To remove it from the display programme would strike a heavy blow at the well-tried recruiting campaign, then vitally important as the standard of aircrew requirements escalated with the advance of both aircraft and tactics.

The importance of the Biggin Hill Show was demonstrated by the decision of the Air Council to reactivate the station for the period of Battle of Britain Week, a costly endeavour since it meant not only detachment of men and women, but the placing of essential equipment such as radar just for a few days flying. A new lease of life was thus provided for the popular nationwide 'At Home Days'. Finally, in 1958 the Government bit the bullet and declared Biggin Hill surplus to requirements, and the following year it became a civil airport.

The opening of Biggin as a civil airport helped to house the light aircraft industry that had been built up at Croydon and which had been sold by the Government to help fund the building of Gatwick Airport. The licensee of the new Biggin Hill Civil Airport was a young ex-fighter pilot who had fought in Korea with the Americans while on exchange posting from the RAF. Squadron Leader Jock Maitland had recently left the Service and saw at once the potential for an airshow so near to London. At that time, 1963, the RAF was still managing to mount the annual September show on the side of the airfield not used by the civil aircraft industry. It was also the time when the British public were beginning to discover the delights of overseas holidays. Only about 3% of the population had flown in a commercial airliner, and the big 'fear' barrier needed to be overcome before the 'package

deal' could set off the 'inclusive-tour' revolution.

Jock Maitland concentrated on introducing his visitors to the airliners in which they would be flying on holidays in the future, and the more enterprising airlines such as British Caledonian gave him full backing. They provided the new airliners, such as the DC7C, for the public to tour round and even fly on for short trips. The air stewardesses in their tartan uniforms roamed the airfield, spreading the gospel and serving the VIPs in the special enclosures. Another supporter was Freddie Laker of British United, the first British airline to fly the new BAC One Elevens. The four days, combining air display, tourist mecca and exhibition park proved to be hugely popular, and became the most successful privately-run air show in the country.

By 1965 the Air Fair at Biggin Hill had become a virtual Trade Show, with light aircraft agents and concessionnaires exhibiting and selling their wares. To add sugar to Jock Maitland's cake, the 'Red Arrows' aerobatic team formed that year and made their first public appearance at Biggin Hill, led by their founder and leader Squadron Leader Lee Jones, an RAF friend of Jock Maitland. Since that date the Red Arrows have always been the premier display at this most innovative show that mixes the best of military display teams with sponsored display items from industry, clubs, and individual aviators of note. Biggin has delighted in giving plenty of airspace to both modern and historic war-birds, genuine and replicas, and to stage aerial 'battles'. Almost all aviators who work and play in this competitive field have at one time or another thrilled the Biggin crowds.

Ever on the prowl for new 'acts', Jock Maitland brought in Concorde to fly along the runway escorted by two Spitfires in 1987, ran a competition for a local girl to ride the top wing of a Tiger Moth and, in 1990, to mark the 75th Anniversary of the British Aerospace factory at Kingston-on-Thames, arranged a formation flypast of a Harrier GR7 and an original 1916 Sopwith Pup that had to be transported by road and assembled at Biggin. The legendary B17 Flying Fortress 'Sally-B' became a Biggin favourite, and when Ted White, the man who brought it to England, died in a Malta air accident, one of the four engine cowlings was painted yellow and black, his racing colours, in his memory.

And so this most famous of RAF stations, Biggin Hill, set the pattern for the two forms of major airshows seen today, the Service-organised and the privately-run. When the RAF decided that it was no longer possible to mount nationwide Battle of Britain Air Shows, they substituted large scale air shows at strategic points in the UK to maintain the traditional support to the Royal Air Force Benevolent Fund and to keep the recruiting message alive.

Perhaps it is a foretaste of the future, at least as far as the RAF is concerned, that Finningley, one of the largest of the stations maintaining independent RAF airshows, is to close and its regional show move to RAF Waddington. The Red Arrows, although so far escaping the political knife, are to move to Marham, as their present base at

Scampton is also to close. The two decisions indicate that, in spite of having to pare expenditure to the bone, the RAF recognises the value of keeping in the public eye, and the potentially devastating effect on recruitment should displays and airshows cease.

After the last war, apart from its regular air shows and the marking of aviation milestones, the RAF ventured to stimulate interest in its future developments, and recruit aircrew, in its own special public air show at Farnborough. The Show, in 1950, was helped by the attendance of HM the King and Queen and other members of the Royal Family, including the two attractive young Princesses. Looking for dramatic publicity just before the Show, the RAF staged one of its events right above Big Ben at Westminster for the benefit of the cameramen. A whole fleet of Harvard trainers were to form the letters 'RAF' to open the Show, and would fly over Westminster on their way to Farnborough. The Press were told that as 11am struck these aerial letters would appear over Parliament, and they did so exactly as Big Ben struck the hour. Pictures of the excellent formation appeared in all the papers, and the team drew much praise from the media for their navigational skills. The Show was a great success, a highlight being the taxying of the Avro trainer used by the King to win his 'wings' during his service with the RAF.

1948 saw The Society of British Aircraft Constructors set up their show at Farnborough, home of the Royal Aircraft Establishment. For the first time the public were admitted on the two weekend days, after four trade days, the pattern that has generally been followed since. SBAC, formed in 1916, held two shows at Olympia jointly with the Aero Club in 1920 and 1929. There had been the first British Aero Show at this venue in 1909, a year before Rolls' death, but that had been part of the Motor Show. SBAC then obtained part use of the New Types Park at the RAF Hendon displays, to which they could invite foreign guests and their own members. They displayed at Hatfield from 1937 for two years, and in 1946 & 47 at Radlett. Now known as Farnborough International, this seven day event begins as a world market place for the aeronautical and space industry and is organised by what is now the Society of British Aerospace Companies. The devotee, the salesman, the purchaser, the spy and the diplomat mingle for five days of entertainment of a high order in marquees, caravans and stands while they inspect weapons of all kinds and see the latest in aircraft technology fly by. The value of this show to the aerospace and weapons industry is incalculable, and aviation is kept in the forefront of the public gaze. On the last two days, a weekend, the show is widened into a public air display with the best of the prototypes handled with dash, and joined by the 'performers' such as the *Red Arrows*.

Farnborough is a unique show and over the years has had many highlights, including the 1958 *Black Arrows* Hunters performing a heart stopping 22 strong loop and 'Roly' Falk slow rolling the giant second prototype Vulcan on Press Day. Two years earlier all three V-bombers were seen together at Farnborough, and Neville Duke arrived in the scarlet Hunter WB188 in which he was much later to regain the World's Speed Record for Britain at 727.6 mph. Then there were such unforgettable sights as the eight- engined Bristol Brabazon, the largest aircraft we have ever built, making its slow and dignified flyby in 1949, the Comet debut in the same year, and the flypast of the ten-engined Saro Princess flying boat, sadly to go the way of Brabazon. There were also tragedies on the way, the worst being in 1952 when John Derry, flying the DH110 at high speed, was killed along with 29 spectators when the aircraft broke up in the air right above the crowds.

With a legacy of 2,600 widows and dependents and 7,500 totally or badly incapacitated officers and men following the first World War, the infant Royal Air Force was determined not to desert them and, in 1919, Lord Trenchard founded a charity that was to become The Royal Air Force Benevolent Fund. The first major contribution above that of regular voluntary donations from the servicemen themselves and the grateful public, came from the Hendon Air Pageant staged in 1920, and since that date all RAF airshows and participation in others by individual elements such as the display aerobatic teams, have as their major aim the support of this most worthy of organisations. The contributions from the few RAF stations still opening their doors, the

efforts of privately run shows such as the Show at Biggin Hill, and the regular donations of loyal supporters were invaluable, but not enough to match the outflow of funds to help the needy.

In 1976 Sir Douglas Bader took over as President of the International Air Tattoo, the object of which was to stage the largest airshow ever with the willing help of our NATO partners and with contributions from other western air arms, indeed from anywhere in the world. That year had been disappointing when it was decided, in the face of the cut-backs throughout Europe, except Russia, to introduce a 'Theme' to make the International Air Tattoo an attraction for international participants as a forum for the exchange of information and for training. The theme in 1976 was a Hunter Meet to mark that aircraft's 25th Anniversary but, disappointingly, among the 27 Hunters that gathered at Greenham Common for the Meet, the only international participant was a Netherlands civilian registered aircraft.

Meanwhile, Sir Douglas, using the same drive and enthusiasm, that had, during the war, fired up unhappy squadrons into leading fighting machines, gathered a team of young publicity and organisationally skilful men and women to produce what is now, clearly, the most exciting display event in Europe. In 1994, for instance, 400 aircraft from 40 countries world-wide came to RAF Fairford, and the display saw nearly forty C130s line up to mark the forty-year service of that remarkable aircraft. Some of the schemes for building up the ultimate 'cake' for the Benevolent Fund were exciting and full of enterprise. Through Goodwood Travel it was possible to fly Concorde to and from the show; for £68.50 you could spoil yourself by becoming a VIP guest in the 'Trenchard' chalet; other enclosures took care of the friends of International Air Tattoo and photo buffs, and in the Trade Fair vast amounts of appropriate gifts and goods were on offer. Nothing was left to chance to make money for the worthy cause and to ensure the comfort of all who supported the endeavour.

There are, of course, dozens of similar airshows, large and small that follow the pattern of Biggin Hill, Finningley and the International Air Tattoo, most making their mark by specialisation, such as the Army Air Corps displays at Middle Wallop and the Royal Naval International Air Day at Yeovilton. Others stage annual nationally supported air races and aerobatic competitions. Then there are the regionally important shows, such as the largest in Scotland staged at RAF Leuchars, superbly located overlooking St. Andrews Bay and the Eden Estuary in Fife. It also has the unique attraction of having its own railway station through which it arranges 'shuttle' services to both north and south on display days. Then, for the real enthusiast there are the air shows that feature either a specific age of flight or aircraft, among which the Shuttleworth Collection at Old Warden, Bedfordshire, is outstanding in running shows and 'Meets' throughout the year. The popularity of these 'Meets' and 'Fly-Ins' is enormous, giving the private flyers the chance to meet and exchange views with their peers. Almost any celebration or anniversary is used as a reason to get airborne and to meet at each other's airfields .

In general, airshows are extremely successful. The public love them and there seems to be a touch of entrepreneurial skill about aviators that enables them to handle the problems and to take the chances without which no outdoor event can succeed. They also have the professional grounding to ensure discipline and safety, whilst arranging unforgettable spectacle for the tens of thousands who attend their shows.

Airshows also provide a place for aviators to meet, to exchange views and anecdotes of past shows. Tales abound, such as that of the VIP at one show who decided to open the event by sailing past the VIP enclosure in the rear seat of a Swordfish. Firing a green flare, he forgot to point it upwards and the flare made a graceful arc into the enclosure, landing on top of a VIP car and stripping off the paint. Then there was the American formation team which flew impressively but very low across Biggin Hill in 1971, creating near pandemonium when they filled the maternity ward of a nearby hospital with coloured smoke. Fairford saw the friendly meeting at the International Tattoo 93 between an RAF Phantom crew and the crew of a Russian *Bear*. They had last met during a live intercept over the North Sea in 1989. Despite the reduction of new aircraft and the size of airforces in Europe, the shows will go on.

IAT95 AIRCRAFT CHECKLIST

THE RAF BENEVOLENT FUND'S INTERNATIONAL AIR TATTOO 95
PARTICIPATING AIRCRAFT

SKYTANKER MEET

Royal Air Force
VC10 C1K	XV104	10 Sqn
VC10 K4	ZD241	101 Sqn
		Highly Commended – Concours d'Elegance
Tristar KC1	ZD953	216 Sqn

Royal Australian Air Force
Boeing 707-338C	A20-627	33 Sqn

Brazilian Air Force
KC-137	2402/02	2/2 GT

Canadian Forces
KCC-130H Hercules	130342	435 Sqn
CC-137	13703	437 Sqn

French Air Force
C-135FR	472/93-CC	ERV 93
C-160NG	F205/64-GE	ET 64

Italian Air Force
Boeing 707	MM62148/14-01	14 Stormo
Tornado	MM7057/36-54	36 Stormo

Royal Saudi Air Force
KC-130H Hercules	3202	32 Sqn
Boeing KE-3A	1816	18 Sqn

South African Air Force
Boeing 707-344	AF617	60 Sqn

United States Air Force
KC-10A Extender	83-0079	305th AMW
KC-135R Stratotanker	64-14837	319th ARW

United States Air Forces Europe
KC-135R Stratotanker	63-8008	100th ARW 'Nightmare'

United States Air Force Reserve
KC-135E Stratotanker	57-1512	452nd AMW 'Bad Boy'
	59-1451	63rd ARS/927th ARW
KC-135R Stratotanker	62-3530	434th AMW

United States Air Force Air National Guard
KC-135E Stratotanker	59-1457	147th ARS/PA ANG
		'Guardian'
		Special mention – Concours d'Elegance
KC-135R Stratotanker	60-0358	136th ARS/NY ANG
	59-1444	166th ARS/OH ANG
		'Spirit of Rickenbacker'
		Overall winner – Concours d'Elegance

United State Marines Corps
KC-130F Hercules	150687/GR-0687	VMGRT-253
KC-130R Hercules	160625/BH-0625	VMGR-252
	160240/QB-0240	VMGR-352

AIRCRAFT IN THE STATIC DISPLAYS (SOUTH SIDE OF AIRFIELD)

Royal Air Force
Bulldog T1	XX619/B	Yorkshire UAS
	XX691/G	Yorkshire UAS
Chinook HC2	ZA709/EQ	7 Sqn
Chipmunk T10	WB550/D	6 AEF
Dominie T1	XS731/J	6 FTS
Gazelle HT3	XW866/E	2 FTS
Harrier GR7	ZD431/02	1 Sqn

Harrier GR7	ZG533/AJ	3 Sqn
	ZG861/AA	3 Sqn
	ZG501	SAOEU/AWC
Harrier GR7 (replica)	'ZG472/01'	EP & TU
Hawk T1	XX172	St Athan Station Flight
Hawk T1A	XX194/CO	100 Sqn
	XX228/CC	100 Sqn
Hawk T1A (replica)	'XX253'	EP & TU
Hawk T1A (replica)	'XX263'	EP & TU
Hercules C3	XV207	LTW
Jaguar GR1A	XX752/EQ	6 Sqn
	XX766/EA	6 Sqn
Jetstream T1	XX482/J	45(R) Sqn
Nimrod MR2	XV251	Kinloss Wing
Puma HC1	XW200	230 Sqn
Sentry AEW1	ZH104	8 Sqn
Tornado F3	ZE291/GQ	43 Sqn
	ZG796/CE	5 Sqn
	ZE340/36-12	56(R) Sqn *(Italian markings)*
Tornado GR1	ZD778/CB	17 Sqn
	ZG771/DW	31 Sqn
	ZD749/U	SAOEU
Tornado GR1A	ZA404/W	2 Sqn
Tornado GR1B	ZA456/AJ-Q	617 Sqn
Tucano T1	ZF417	1 FTS
Wessex HC2	XR505/WA	2 FTS
	XR511/L	60 Sqn

Royal Navy
Gazelle HT2	XZ942/CU-42	705 NAS/*Sharks*
Hawk T1A	XX346	FRADU
Jetstream T2	XX487/CU-568	750 NAS
Sea King HAR5	XV666/CU-823	771 NAS
Sea King HC4	ZE425/26	772 NAS

Ministry of Defence (Procurement Executive)
Andover C1PR	XS596	A&AEE 'UK OPEN SKIES'
Canberra B2	WH734	DTEO Llanbedr
Harrier T10	ZH654	A&AEE
Harvard IIB	FT375	A&AEE
	KF183	A&AEE
Hawk T1	XX154	DTEO Llanbedr
	XX343/3	ETPS
Hawk T1 ASTRA	XX341/1	ETPS
Hunter FGA9	XE601	A&AEE
Hunter T7	XL612/2	ETPS
Jaguar T2A	ZB615	A&AEE

Belgian Air Force
Alpha Jet	AT 31	7 Sml

Bulgarian Air Force
Tu-134A *Crusty*	LZ D 050	16 TAB

Czech Air Force
Mil Mi-24V *Hind*	4011	331 Sqn
Antonov An-26 *Curl*	2409	344 Sqn
Antonov An-30 *Clank*	1107	344 Sqn *'OPEN SKIES'*

Royal Danish Air Force
C-130H Hercules	B-680	Esk 721
F-16B Fighting Falcon	ET-197	Esk 726
	ET-199	Esk 726
Gulfstream III	F-313	Esk 721
T-17 Supporter	T-405	FSNKAR
	T-426	FLSK

Royal Danish Navy
Lynx Mk80	S-142	Esk 722
S-61A Sea King	U-277	Esk 722

Royal Danish Army
Hughes 500M	H-244	RDAAC 2
SA550C-2 Fennec	P-369	RDAAC 1
	P-287	RDAAC 1 (VIP Flight)

Finnish Air Force
Hawk Mk 51A	HW315/T	Kou1LLV

French Navy
Atlantique NG	17	21F
Falcon 10 (MER)	143	57S
Super Frelon	164	32F

French Army Light Aviation
AS532 Super Puma/ Cougar	2282/AIS	4 RHCM
Cessna F406 Caravan II	0010/ABN	3 GHL
SA330 Puma	1198/ARH/71	4 RHCM

German Air Force
Alpha Jet	41+09	FLG
C-160D Transall	50+06	LTG-63
F-4F Phantom	37+38	JG-73
MiG-29A	29+08	JG-73
Tornado IDS	45+04	JbG-33
	43+13	JbG-33

German Army
Sikorsky CH-53G	84+84	HFTR-15
MBB Bo 105M	80+24	HFTR-15

German Navy
Atlantic	61+14	MFG-3
Do228	57+01	MFG-5
Sea King Mk41	89+67	MFG-5
Tornado IDS	46+20	MFG-2

Italian Air Force
Atlantic	MM40118/30-03	30 Stormo
TF-104G Starfighter	MM54251/4-34	4 Stormo
	MM54261/4-42	4 Stormo
Aermacchi MB339A	MM54463/61-17	61 Stormo
	MM54496/61-42	61 Stormo
	MM54473/4	*Frecce Tricolori*

Italian Army
Agusta-Bell AB 412	MM81360/E.I.469	49 GSEA/5 RIGEL
Agusta A109AII	MM81250/E.I.873	49 GSEA/5 RIGEL

Royal Jordanian Air Force
C-130H Hercules	346	3 Sqn

NATO
Boeing 707-329C	LX-N19996	NAEWF
E-3A	LX-N90443	NAEWF

Royal Netherlands Air Force
Agusta-Bell AB 412	R-03	SAR Flight
Alouette III	A-536	302 Sqn
F-16A Fighting Falcon	J-021	312 Sqn
F-16B Fighting Falcon	J-068	312 Sqn
MBB Bo 105CB	B-78	299 Sqn

Royal Netherlands Navy
SH-14D Lynx	278	7 Sqn
P-3C Orion	304	320 Sqn/MARPAT

Royal New Zealand Air Force
C-130H Hercules	NZ7004	40 Sqn

Royal Norwegian Air Force
Falcon 20ECM	041	717 Skv
Twin Otter	7057	719 Skv

Polish Air Force
Antonov An-26 *Curl*	SP-KWC	13 PLT

Portuguese Air Force
TA-7P Corsair	15546	Esc 302/304
C-130H-30 Hercules	16806	Esc 501

Royal Saudi Air Force
Tornado IDS	762	7 Sqn

Slovak Air Force
MiG-29UB *Fulcrum*	1303	1 Sqn/31 Air Base Wing
L-39 Albatros	0442/0	*White Albatros*
Antonov An-12 *Cub*	2209	1 Sqn/32 Air Base Wing

Spanish Air Force
C-130H Hercules	T.10-04/31-04	Ala 31

Swedish Air Force
Saab AJS37 Viggen	37057/57	F7
Saab SF37 Viggen	37976/38/976	F7
Saab Tp 100	100001/001	F16
C-130E/Tp 84 Hercules	84001/841	F7

Swiss Air Force
Hunter F58	J-4025	*Patrouille Suisse*

Turkish Air Force
C-130E Hercules	13186/12-186	222 Filo
F-4E Phantom	67-0298/1-298	112 Filo
	67-0395/1-395	112 Filo

United States Air Force
B-1B Lancer	86-0094/EL	37thBS/28th BW
B-52H Stratofortress	60-0058/MT	23rd BS/5th BW
C-5B Galaxy	87-0031	436th AW
C-130H Hercules	92-0550/LK	50th AS/314th AW
U-2R	80-1092/BB	9th RW/OL (UK)

United States Air Forces Europe
A-10A Thunderbolt II	81-0962/SP	81st FS/52nd FW
	81-0984/SP	81st FS/52nd FW
C-9A Nightingale	71-0880	75th AS/86th Wing
C-21A Learjet	84-0108	76th AS/86th Wing
	84-0082	HQ USEUCOM
C-130E Hercules	70-1271	86th Wing
HC-130N Hercules	69-5823	67th SOS/352nd SOG
F-15C Eagle	86-0176/LN	493rd FS/48th FW
F-15E Eagle	90-0248/LN	48th FW
F-16C Fighting Falcon	88-0413/AV	510th FS/31st FW
	89-0009/AV	555th FS/31st FW

United States Air Force Reserve
B-52H Stratofortress	61-0029/BD	93rd BS
C-141B Starlifter	66-0201	452nd AMW

United States Air Force Air National Guard
C-130H Hercules	90-1798	164th ALS/179th AG 'Spirit of Shelby'
EC-130E Hercules	63-7773	193rd SOS/PA ANG

United States Army
Beech C-12C	76-22549	USEUCOM Flight
Beech RC-12K	85-0155	1st MIB
UH-1H Iroquois	74-22513	USEUCOM
CH-47D Chinook	87-0073	A Co.5/159th Avn
UH-60A Black Hawk	88-26083	C Co.7/158th Avn
AH-64A Apache	86-8941	ATNB 6-6 Cav

United States Navy
F/A-18C Hornet	164657/AJ-405	VFA-87

IAT95 AIRCRAFT CHECKLIST

Civilian

BAe 125-800B	N98	FAA
BAe Hawk 102D	ZJ100	British Aerospace
BAe Hawk 200 (replica)		British Aerospace
BN-2T Islander	G-BVHX	Pilatus Britten-Norman
Buccaneer S.2 (nose)	XV353	
CFM Shadow	G-MYLV	
Defender 4000	G-SURV	Pilatus Britten-Norman
DH Sea Devon C20	XK895/CU-19 (G-SDEV)	Peter Gill
DH Dragon Rapide	G-AEML	Proteus Holdings
DH Vampire T.55	U-1219 (G-DHWW)	Source Classic Flight
HS Gnat T1	'XM693' (G-TIMM)	Kennet Aviation
Jet Provost T1	G-AOBU	Kennet Aviation
Jet Provost T5	XS230 (G-BVWF)	Transair (UK) Ltd
Let L-410UVP	SP-TXB	(Sat only, dep Sun)
PA-28 Arrow IV	G-BUUM	(Sat only)
PA-28 Warrior	G-BRTX	(Sat only)
PA-28 Cherokee 140	G-DIAT	Avon Aviation/RAFBF
Short Skyvan	LX-JUL	Hunting Aviation
Whirlwind HAR10	XJ729 (G-BVGE)	Austen Associates

AIRCRAFT IN THE FLYING DISPLAY (AND SPARES) ON FLIGHTLINES (NORTH SIDE)

Royal Air Force

Harrier GR7	ZD329/H	20(R) Sqn
	ZD409/B	20(R) Sqn
Hawk T1	XX235	19(R) Sqn
	XX244	19(R) Sqn
Jaguar GR1A	XX116	16(R) Sqn
Nimrod MR2	XV232	Kinloss Wing
Tornado F3	ZE732/AS	56(R) Sqn
	ZE790/AO	56(R) Sqn
Tornado GR1	ZA327/B-51	TTTE
	ZA560	TTTE
Tornado GR1A	ZE116/O	2 Sqn
Tucano T1	ZF406	1 FTS
	ZF514	1 FTS
Wessex HC2	XT601	22 Sqn

Royal Navy

Gazelle HT2	XW853/CU-53	705 NAS *Sharks*
	XW864/CU-54	705 NAS *Sharks*
	XX436/CU-39	705 NAS *Sharks*
	XX451/CU-58	705 NAS *Sharks*
Sea King HAS6	XV663/CU-501	810 NAS
	ZD634/CU-506	810 NAS

Army Air Corps

Gazelle AH1	XW865	*Blue Eagles*
	XW908	*Blue Eagles*
	XX375	*Blue Eagles*
	ZA726	*Blue Eagles*
	ZA737	*Blue Eagles*
Lynx AH7	ZD278/A	*Blue Eagles*

Czech Air Force

Mil Mi-24V *Hind*	0702	331 Sqn
	0703	331 Sqn
	0709	331 Sqn
Sukhoi Su-22M-4 *Fitter*	3802/26	321 Sqn/2 Wing
	4006/31	321 Sqn/2 Wing
	4007/32	321 Sqn/2 Wing
	4010/28	321 Sqn/2 Wing
	4209/54	321 Sqn/2 Wing
Sukhoi Su-22UM-3K	7310/25	321 Sqn/2 Wing

French Air Force

Alpha Jet E (Displayed Sat only)	E37/1 (F-TERI)	*Patrouille de France*
	E97/2 (F-TERL)	*Patrouille de France*
	E105/3 (F-TERF)	*Patrouille de France*
	E106/4 (F-TERJ)	*Patrouille de France*
	E125/5 (F-TERH)	*Patrouille de France*
	E140/6 (F-TERD)	*Patrouille de France*
	E132/7 (F-TERN)	*Patrouille de France*
	E72/8 (F-TERG)	*Patrouille de France*
	E23/9 (F-TERO)	*Patrouille de France*
	E173/0 (F-TERP)	*Patrouille de France*
C-160NG Transall	F208/64-GH	ET/64
Mirage 2000B	511/2-FH	EC2/2
Mirage 2000C	18/2-FL	EC2/2

French Navy

Lynx HAS2(FN)	623	34F

French Army Air Corps

SA342M Gazelle	4166/CXA	1 RHC

German Air Force

UH-1D	71+73	LTG-62

German Navy

Tornado IDS	45+13	MFG-2 (Sat only)
	45+36	MFG-2

Italian Air Force

Aermacchi MB339PAN (Displayed Sun only)	MM54439/6	*Frecce Tricolori*
	MM54445/8	*Frecce Tricolori*
	MM54475/1	*Frecce Tricolori*
	MM54477/9	*Frecce Tricolori*
	MM54480/0	*Frecce Tricolori*
	MM54482/5	*Frecce Tricolori*
	MM54483/13	*Frecce Tricolori*
	MM54484/3	*Frecce Tricolori*
	MM54486/2	*Frecce Tricolori*
	MM54536/10	*Frecce Tricolori*
Aeritalia G222	MM62130/RS-51	RSV
AMX Centaur	MM7131/RS-13	RSV

Italian Army

Agusta A129	MM81398/E.I.928	49 GSEA/5 RIGEL

Royal Moroccan Air Force

CAP 231 (Displayed Sun only)	CN-ABI/06	*Marche Verte*
	CN-ABJ/07	*Marche Verte*
	CN-ABL/09	*Marche Verte*
	CN-ABM/22	*Marche Verte*
	CN-ABN/23	*Marche Verte*
	CN-ABO/24	*Marche Verte*
CASA/IPTN CN 235	CNA-MB	3rd Base

Royal Netherlands Air Force

Alouette III	A-324	*Grasshoppers*
	A-350	*Grasshoppers*
	A-390	*Grasshoppers*
	A-398	*Grasshoppers*
	A-453	*Grasshoppers*
Pilatus PC-7	L-02	EMVO
	L-09	EMVO
F-16A Fighting Falcon	J-508	311 Sqn
	J-019	312 Sqn
	J-011	315 Sqn
F-16B Fighting Falcon	J-884	315 Sqn

Royal Norwegian Air Force

F-5A	208	336 Skv
	902	336 Skv
F-5B	907	336 Skv
	908	336 Skv

Polish Air Force

Antonov An-26 *Curl*	SP-LWA	13 PLT
PZL Mielec TS-11 Iskra	210/7	*White Iskras*
(Displayed Sat only)	510/9	*White Iskras*
	702/3	*White Iskras*
	709/8	*White Iskras*
	713/5	*White Iskras*
	714/6	*White Iskras*
	726/2	*White Iskras*
	730/1	*White Iskras*
	827/10	*White Iskras*
	1010/4	*White Iskras*

Slovak Air Force

MiG-29A *Fulcrum*	0619	1 Sqn/31 Air Base Wing
L-39C Albatros	0101/4	*White Albatros*
(Displayed Sun only)	0102/6	*White Albatros*
	0111/5	*White Albatros*
	0112/1	*White Albatros*
	0443/7	*White Albatros*
	4355/3	*White Albatros*
	4357/2	*White Albatros*

Spanish Air Force

CASA C101ED Aviojet	E25-06/79-06/8	*Patrulla Aguila*
(Displayed Sat only)	E25-08/79-08/1	*Patrulla Aguila*
	E25-13/79-13/3	*Patrulla Aguila*
	E25-22/79-22/7	*Patrulla Aguila*
	E25-23/79-23/4	*Patrulla Aguila*
	E25-25/79-25/5	*Patrulla Aguila*
	E25-27/79-27/6	*Patrulla Aguila*
	E25-40/79-40/2	*Patrulla Aguila*

Royal Swedish Air Force

Saab SF37 Viggen	37954/30	F7
	37962/36	F7

Swiss Air Force

Northrop F-5E	J-3080	*Patrouille Suisse*
	J-3081	*Patrouille Suisse*
	J-3085	*Patrouille Suisse*
	J-3086	*Patrouille Suisse*
	J-3087	*Patrouille Suisse*
	J-3088	*Patrouille Suisse*
	J-3091	*Patrouille Suisse*
Learjet 35A	T-782	Dubendorf SF (Sat only)

United States Air Force

B-1B Lancer	85-0084/EL	37th BS/28th BW

United States Air Forces Europe

F-16C Fighting Falcon	90-0813/SP	22nd FS/52nd FW
	91-0338/SP	22nd FS/52nd FW

Civilian

Avro 504N	H5199 (G-ADEV)	Shuttleworth Trust
Avro Tutor	K3215 (G-AHSA)	Shuttleworth Trust
Bell 206 Jet Ranger	G-BKEW	Lynton Aviation
Bristol Blenheim IV	Z5722 (G-BPIV)	British Aerial Museum
Extra 300	JY-RNA	*Royal Jordanian Falcons*
(Displayed Sun only)	JY-RNB	*Royal Jordanian Falcons*
	JY-RND	*Royal Jordanian Falcons*
	JY-RNE	*Royal Jordanian Falcons*
Flycatcher (replica)	'S1287/5' (G-BEYB)	John Fairey
Gloster Gladiator I	N2308/HP-B (G-AMRK)	Shuttleworth Trust
Hawker Hind	K5414 (G-AENP)	Shuttleworth Trust
Jet Provost T.3A	XN461/28 (G-BVBE)	Jet Provost Club
MBB BO 105D	G-AZOR	Bond Helicopters
MBB Bo 105DBS/4	G-BUXS	Police
RAF SE5A	F904 (G-EBIA)	Shuttleworth Trust
Westland Lysander IIIA	2442/MA-D (OO-SOT)	SABENA Old Timers

FLYING DISPLAY AIRCRAFT (DID NOT LAND) SATURDAY 30 JULY AND SUNDAY 31 JULY

Antonov An-2	HA-MEP	St Ivel (Landed Sun)
Stearman A75N1	N707TJ/2	Crunchie Flying Circus
Stearman PT-13D	N5057V/1	Crunchie Flying Circus
Fairey Swordfish II	W5856/A2-A	RN Historic Flt (Sat only)
	LS326/LZ	RN Historic Flt (Sun only)
DH115 Vampire FB6	'109' (G-BVPO)	R Jord AF Historic Flight
DH115 Vampire T55	(G-BVLM)	R Jord AF Historic Flight
Hawker Hunter T7	'800/F' (G-BOOM)	R Jord AF Historic Flight
DH 82A Tiger Moth	G-ADGV	
(All landed Sat & Sun)	G-ADXT	
	G-AGEG	(Sun only)
	G-AGZZ	
	G-AKXS	(Sat only)
	G-ANFM	
	G-ANLD	
	G-ANRN	
	G-BPAJ	
	DE992 (G-AXXV)	
	DF128/RCO-U	(G-AOJJ)
	N6847 (G-APAL)	
	T5424 (G-AJOA)	(Sat only)
	A17-48 (G-BPHR)	(Sun only)
Tristar C2	ZE706	RAF 216 Sqn (Sat only)
	ZE705	RAF 216 Sqn (Sun only)
VC10 C1K	XV103	RAF 10 Sqn
VC10 K2	ZA143/D	RAF 101 Sqn
VC10 K3	ZA149	RAF 101 Sqn
VC10 K4	ZD240/M	RAF 101 Sqn
Harrier GR7	ZD323/05	RAF 1 Sqn
	ZD461/WH	RAF 1 Sqn
	ZD470/01	RAF 1 Sqn (Sat only)
	ZG860/08	RAF 1 Sqn (Sat only)
	ZD462/07	RAF 1 Sqn (Sun only)
	ZD464/09	RAF 1 Sqn (Sun only)
Hercules C1	XV185	RAF LTW
	XV195	RAF LTW
	XV210	RAF LTW (Landed)
	XV215	RAF LTW (Landed)
Hercules C1K	XV203	RAF LTW
Hercules C3	XV212	RAF LTW
	XV217	RAF LTW
Hawk T1	XX237	RAF *Red Arrows*
	XX294	RAF *Red Arrows*
	XX307	RAF *Red Arrows*
	XX308	RAF *Red Arrows*
Hawk T1A	XX252	RAF *Red Arrows*
	XX253	RAF *Red Arrows*
	XX260	RAF *Red Arrows*
	XX266	RAF *Red Arrows*
	XX306	RAF *Red Arrows*
Eurofighter 2000	ZH558	British Aerospace
Extra 300	G-HIII	Rover Display Team
	G-SIII	Rover Display Team
Spitfire Vb	AB910/AE-H	RAF BBMF
Hurricane IIC	PZ865/J	RAF BBMF
Lancaster B1	PA474/WS-J	RAF BBMF
Mosquito T3	RR299/HT-E (G-ASKH)	British Aerospace
P-38J Lightning	67543/KI-S (NX3145X)	The Fighter Collection
P-47D/N Thunderbolt	'226671' (NX47DD)	The Fighter Collection
P-51D Mustang	'463221' (N51JJ)	The Fighter Collection
B-17G Flying Fortress	'124485' (G-BEDF)	B-17 Preservation
Tornado IDS	44+63	German AF JBG-33
	44+84	German AF JBG-33
	45+08	German AF JBG-33
	45+17	German AF JBG-33
Hawk T1	XX173	RAF 6 FTS
	XX238	RAF 6 FTS